WHERE ARE THE CHRISTIANS?

I0806873

ISBN 13: 978-1-4621-1293-7

Published by Plain Sight Publishing, an imprint of Cedar Fort, Inc.
2373 W. 700 S., Springville, UT 84663
Distributed by Cedar Fort, Inc., www.cedarfort.com

The Library of Congress has catalogued the companion volume, *Where Are the Christians? The Unrealized Potential of a Divided Religion*, as follows:

Shuster, Eric, 1962- author.
Where are the Christians? : the unrealized potential of a divided religion / By Eric Shuster.
pages cm
Includes bibliographical references.
ISBN 978-1-4621-1206-7 (alk. paper)
1. Christian union. 2. Church--Unity. I. Title.

BX8.3.S53 2013
262.001'1--dc23

2013002992

Cover design by Angela D. Olsen
Cover design © 2013 by Lyle Mortimer
Edited and typeset by Whitney A. Lindsley

Printed in the United States of America

10 9 8 7 6 5 4 3 2 1

WHERE ARE THE CHRISTIANS?

COMPANION WORKBOOK

ERIC SHUSTER

PLAIN SIGHT PUBLISHING
AN IMPRINT OF CEDAR FORT, INC.
SPRINGVILLE, UTAH

CONTENTS

BEFORE BEGINNING YOUR EXPEDITION

Jesus Christ is from "everlasting to everlasting," yet Christianity as a religion has only been around for about two thousand years. Your Christianity began when you accepted Jesus Christ as your personal Savior and made a conscious decision to become a Christian (Romans 10:9). For some churches, there are rituals associated with becoming a Christian, such as baptism, bearing testimony, or answering an altar call. Reflecting on the journey from the point that you became a Christian to this very moment, you need to ask yourself, "What kind of Christian have I become?" Although this question is difficult to answer objectively, indicators of belief and practice can identify you along the Christian Continuum (explained later), helping you *find your Christianity.* To find your Christianity means embarking on a personal expedition to explore your thoughts and feelings and to examine the "fleshy tables" of your heart (2 Corinthians 3:3).

The purpose of this workbook is to help you navigate the expedition to find your Christianity and to provide a framework for study and reflection. Whether you are using this workbook by yourself or joining with a group of others in a workshop, the goal of your expedition is to locate where you are on the narrow path of Christianity (Matthew 7:14) and to understand better how the gospel of Jesus Christ can be more fully applied in your life. By accomplishing these things, you can reach your spiritual potential and obtain greater peace and joy in your journey as a Christian.

This workbook is a companion to the book *Where Are the Christians? The Unrealized Potential of a Divided Religion.* If you have read the book, then you will have some additional markers to direct you on your expedition; however, this workbook assumes you have not read the book and therefore summarizes for your benefit the principles that are laid out in more detail in *Where Are the Christians?*

WHAT YOU'LL NEED FOR THE EXPEDITION

Besides this workbook, you will need four other things to make this trip more enjoyable:

1. **A Bible:** This workbook includes a substantial number of biblical references using the King James translation. Some of the references provide the entire verse, others a portion of the verse, and others only the reference itself. Having a Bible handy, especially if it is your personal Bible in which you can make notations and highlights, will make the experience more productive and fulfilling.

2. **A Pen or Pencil:** This expedition is interactive. The workbook will give you ideas to consider and ask you to write down your own thoughts and feelings just as you would in a journal. When you see the heading "Diary of Thoughts," that will indicate that it is time to write and record what is being asked of you. At the end of your expedition, these recorded thoughts will be a useful diary to reference and use as a guide in your quest toward a more fulfilling discipleship in the gospel of Jesus Christ.

3. **The book *Where Are the Christians? The Unrealized Potential of a Divided Religion*:** Although not a requirement to have read beforehand, having a copy handy will help explain in more detail some of the principles introduced.

4. **Commitment:** The old adage "you only get out of something what you put into it" is certainly true in this instance. This workbook will cover some deep subjects and ask you to objectively reflect upon and respond to questions about your beliefs and practices as a Christian. Your personal commitment to being honest with yourself and determined in the quest will ensure you get the most out of not only this experience but also your entire life's journey as a Christian.

Our expedition will cover eight chapters and a variety of activities—here is the map:

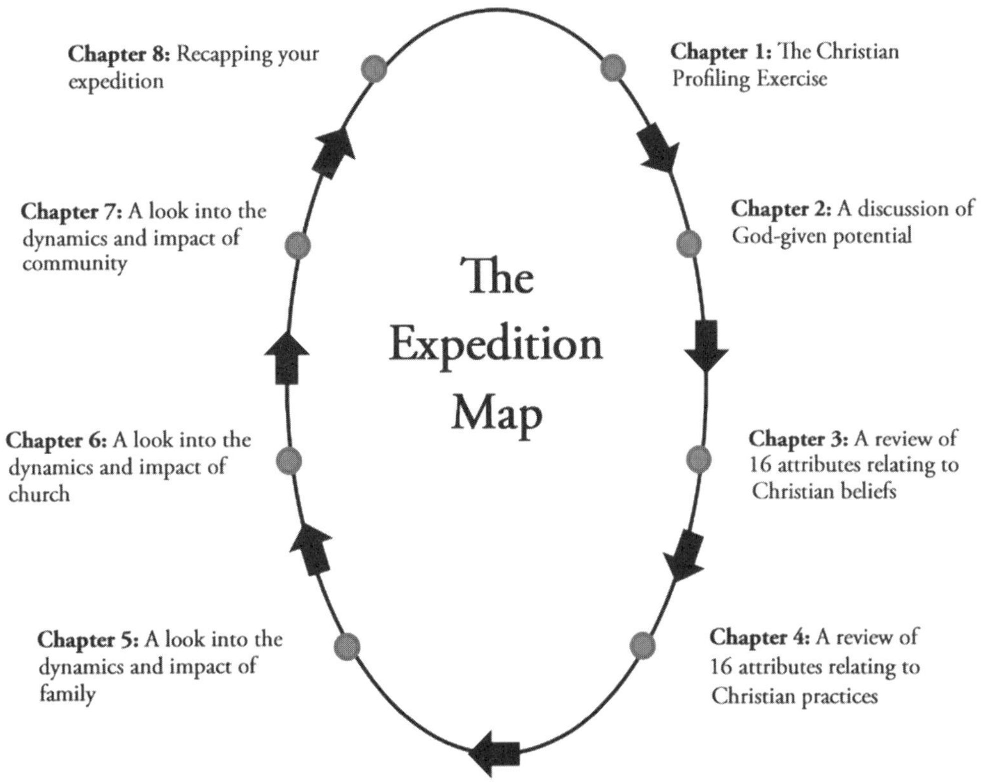

Diagram 1: Expedition Map

Now that you know what to expect and you've packed your things, let's get moving. Pause for a moment to say a prayer asking the Lord to provide you with the guidance of the Holy Ghost and to bless you on this exciting voyage to find your Christianity—or at least discover a side of your Christianity that you may not have explored before this time. As is often said to those about to embark on a long and arduous expedition—Godspeed!

A NOTE TO GROUP FACILITATORS

If you are facilitating a group session using this workbook, you may want to consider tailoring four areas of the workbook to your group:

1. **Church Doctrine:** The Christian doctrines outlined in this workbook are referred to generally, allowing you the ability to elaborate according to your church's specific theological foundation.

2. **Church Culture:** The materials in this workbook are structured to be adaptable to the various lifestyles, attitudes, and life experiences of group members.

3. **Facilitator Style:** You probably have a style of teaching you are most comfortable with and this workbook allows for great flexibility in working with your personal teaching style.

4. **Divine Inspiration:** Ultimately your goal is to be guided by the Holy Ghost. By doing so, you will be directed to teach this material in the most effective way for your students. Above all, let divine inspiration be your guide.

To save time with respect to the Christian profiling activity in chapter one, it is recommended that students complete the exercise at www.findyourchristianity.com beforehand and bring the results with them to your session. May the Lord be with you as you help facilitate your students on their expedition to find their Christianity.

Chapter 1

THE CHRISTIAN PROFILING EXERCISE

A Christian's level of faith changes throughout his or her lifetime in an often erratic and volatile way. A Christian might be inactive and disillusioned, only to be inspired by a life-changing event that increases his or her faith toward becoming a more active and vibrant Christian. Conversely, he or she might be active and faithful, only to lose interest and become a more inactive and indolent Christian. All of us experience large or small gyrations of spirituality depending on the amount of faith and effort we put into our spiritual lives.

In general, there are two types of Christians:

Believing Christian

A *Believing Christian* is one who believes in and accepts the divinity of Jesus Christ as the Only Begotten Son of God, the one true Messiah, and the only pathway to the forgiveness of sin, salvation, and eternal life through the grace of God the Father.

Practicing Christian

A *Practicing Christian* is a Believing Christian who commits to living the precepts of the Church they belong to, including repentance, baptism, receiving the gift of the Holy Ghost, and partaking of the Lord's Supper—motivating them to keep the commandments, follow the example of Jesus Christ, make sacrifices in building and nurturing the kingdom of God, perform good works, and live a life embodying Christian values.

Diagram 2 provides a summary of the dynamics between a Believing and Practicing Christian, called the Christian Discipleship Model. Notice the transition between a Believing Christian and a Practicing Christian is bridged by the degree of personal conversion one has in committing to the gospel of Jesus Christ:

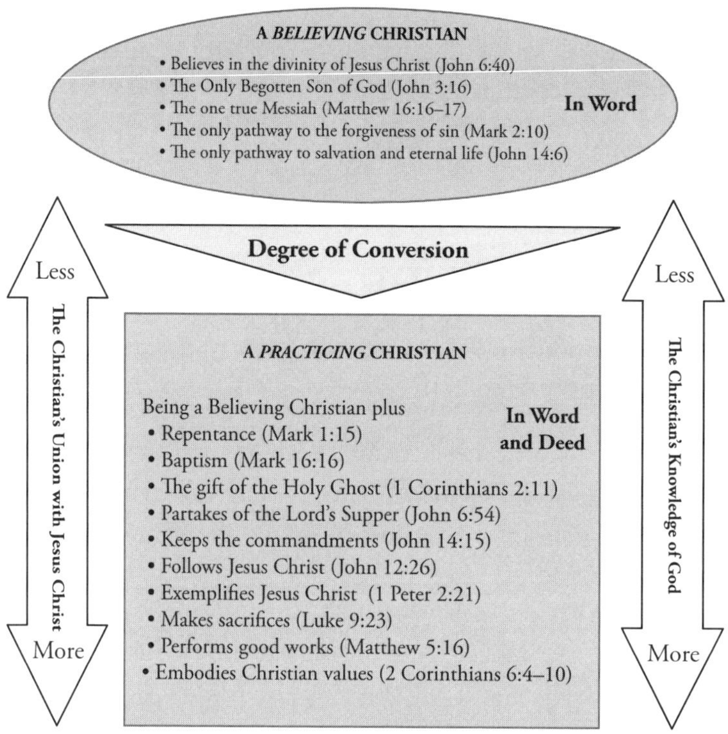

Diagram 2: The Model of Christian Discipleship

The two integrated definitions of a Believing and Practicing Christian are useful but lack the specifics to help us understand more granularly what type of Christian we are. To aid us in our understanding, there exists what we will call the *Christian Continuum*, along which there are five types of Christians (four are common and the fifth we will cover later). Diagram 3 shows the Christian Continuum and the four common Christian types:

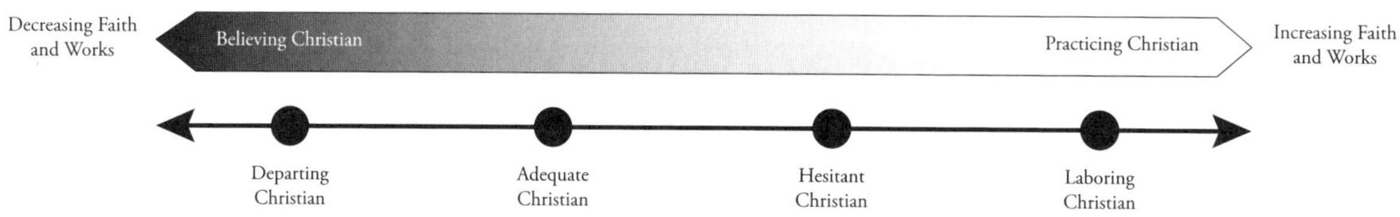

Diagram 3: The Christian Continuum

The following are brief single-sentence descriptions of the four most common Christians, which will be explained in more detail later in the chapter:

- **Departing Christians:** These are individuals who have lost (or nearly lost) their testimony of Jesus Christ, are fairly inactive in their church, and are not sure if they consider themselves to be Christians any longer.
- **Adequate Christians:** These are the "average Christians"—those who feel they have enough faith and exercise enough works and are therefore not proactively doing anything to grow spiritually as Christians.
- **Hesitant Christians:** These are Christians with great faith in Jesus Christ and his gospel, but who "hesitate" to make sacrifices in doing good works, including witnessing of Christ to others, helping the poor, and actively seeking out ways of serving in love.
- **Laboring Christians:** These are Christians with great faith in Jesus Christ and his gospel who do all they can to exemplify discipleship by actively serving others, making sacrifices, and continuously nurturing their testimony in the scriptures and in prayer.

Diary of Thoughts

Which type of Christian do you consider yourself to be and why?

THE CHRISTIAN PROFILING EXERCISE

Chances are, you can come close to pinpointing where you are along the Christian Continuum yourself. However, to make the exercise more fun, the Christian Profiling Exercise was created. The exercise can accurately identify what kind of Christian you are right now. The three-part exercise consists of a series of questions based on your faith and practice as a Christian. The questions are answered on a rating scale of 1 to 5 based upon the **level of agreement** you have with the particular statement:

5 = completely agree

4 = agree

3 = somewhat agree

2 = disagree

1 = completely disagree

- **Part One:** Part one evaluates your belief (or faith) on a primary set of five Believing Christian attributes.
- **Part Two:** Part two evaluates your beliefs on a secondary set of Believing Christian attributes. These eleven attributes are meant to measure the depth of your belief using tenets that are closely associated with faith in God the Father, the Holy Ghost, and Jesus Christ according to the Model of Christian Discipleship (see Diagram 2).
- **Part Three:** Part three evaluates your practice (or works) on a set of sixteen Practicing Christian attributes.

After completing the exercise, you will be able to use your scores to easily identify what kind of Christian you are. If you want to bypass filling out the manual survey in this workbook, you can go to the Christian Profiling Exercise at www.findyourchristianity.com and complete the exercise online. The online version will allow you to print the results, making things a bit easier for you.

A Word about Honesty in Completing the Exercise

We all have aspirations as to the type of people we want to be. Oftentimes these aspirations do not accurately reflect the people we are in the present. The Christian Profiling Exercise is meant to measure your belief and practice at the moment the exercise is completed, not what you would like it to be in the future. For you to get the most out of this exercise, you must answer each question with complete honesty and with reference to your current state. Should you decide to sneak in a bit of "hopeful thinking," your Christian profile will not be accurate. Psalm 51:6 states, "Behold, thou desirest truth in the inward parts: and in the hidden part thou shalt make me to know wisdom," meaning it is important that you be honest with yourself because by doing so you will reap wisdom.

Are you ready? Answer the 32 questions using the 1 to 5 level of agreement ratings explained earlier: 5 = completely agree; 4 = agree; 3 = somewhat agree; 2 = disagree; 1 = completely disagree:

PART ONE AND TWO: BELIEVING CHRISTIAN ATTRIBUTES

PART ONE: Believing Christian Attributes—Primary	1	2	3	4	5
1. Jesus Christ is the only true Messiah, the Savior of the world					
2. Jesus Christ is the Only Begotten Son of God					
3. Jesus Christ is the only way to the forgiveness of sins					
4. Jesus Christ is the only way to everlasting life (salvation)					
5. Jesus Christ is the only way to God the Father					
Primary Believing Score (add up your answers 1 through 5)					

Table 1: Christian Profiling Exercise *Part One*, Primary Believing Attributes

PART TWO: Believing Christian Attributes—Secondary	1	2	3	4	5
6. God is our Heavenly Father (the Father of our spirits)					
7. God the Father and Jesus Christ are one					
8. God the Father makes all things possible					
9. The Holy Ghost is one in purpose with, and proceeds from, God the Father being active in the lives of the faithful					
10. The Holy Ghost provides comfort and knowledge from God					
11. All humans suffer from sin requiring repentance to receive forgiveness					
12. Baptism is a spiritual cleansing and gateway into the Church of Jesus Christ					
13. The Lord's Supper symbolizes a remembrance of Christ's sacrifice if you are a Protestant or a Mormon, or is the literal body and blood of Jesus Christ (Eucharist) if you are a Catholic					
14. The scriptures (for example, the Bible) are the inspired word of God					
15. You are able to believe without seeing in spiritual matters as one having faith (that is, you don't need to be given divine evidence)					
16. You consider yourself to be born again, converted, with a new life in Jesus Christ					
Secondary Believing Score (add up your answers 6 through 16)					

Table 2: Christian Profiling Exercise *Part Two*, Secondary Believing Attributes

Now add up both your primary and secondary believing scores:

Primary Believing Score from Table 1	
Secondary Believing Score from Table 2	
TOTAL Believing Score	

Table 3: Christian Profiling Exercise: Total Believing Score

Adding the primary believing score from part one with the secondary believing score from part two in table 3 determines your total believing score for the exercise. Set this score aside while you tackle the next section.

PART THREE: PRACTICING CHRISTIAN ATTRIBUTES

The questions in this exercise are rated on the same agreement scale used in parts one and two and measure your intentions and effort in living the sixteen practicing attributes. There are two words that need further defining before you can complete part three of the exercise—"strive" and "regularly":

- **Strive:** "strive" means you exert an ever-conscious and vigorous effort to live the principle, as opposed to having good intentions that exists in the background of your life.
- **Regularly:** "regularly" means it is part of a cultivated discipline of consistent behavior in your life, demonstrating a commitment to the principle as opposed to a "when I have time" type of behavior.

Ready for part three? Answer the 32 questions using the 1 to 5 level of agreement ratings explained earlier: 5 = completely agree; 4 = agree; 3 = somewhat agree; 2 = disagree; 1 = completely disagree:

PART THREE: Practicing Christian Attributes	**1**	**2**	**3**	**4**	**5**
1. You strive to keep all of the commandments of God and the teachings of his Son Jesus Christ					
2. You regularly repent, asking for forgiveness of and turning away from sin					
3. You regularly pray to God the Father—out loud, in private, and/or even within your heart					
4. You strive to follow the teachings and example of Jesus Christ					
5. You regularly make meaningful personal sacrifices in living the gospel of Jesus Christ					

6. You regularly perform service for others spending your own personal time to do so					
7. You regularly share the gospel of Jesus Christ with others					
8. You strive to be pure in heart including earnest attempts to exercise humility, having gratitude in the Lord					
9. You regularly give of your time, talents, and substance to others					
10. You regularly praise God and his Son Jesus Christ in worship					
11. You strive to love others in kindness and charity					
12. You strive to be a good example of Christian values and living					
13. You regularly read and study the scriptures (for example, the Bible)					
14. You regularly fellowship with other Christians in worship					
15. You strive to actively forgive and show mercy to others					
16. You strive to be a peacemaker among those with whom you associate					
Total Practicing Score (add up your answers 1 through 16)					

Table 4: Christian Profiling Exercise *Part Three*, Practicing Christian Attributes

IDENTIFYING YOUR CHRISTIAN TYPE

After completing each of the three parts of the exercise, you are ready to identify your Christian type by plotting your *total* Believing Score and your *total* Practicing Score on diagram 4 below:

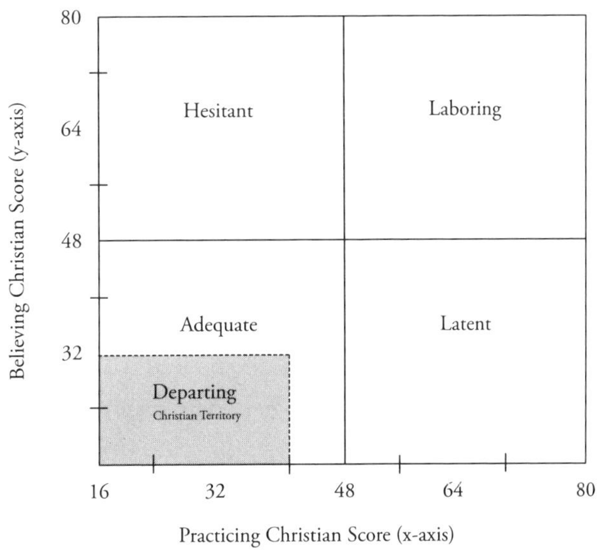

Diagram 4: The Christian Profiling Matrix

The plot begins by locating your Believing Christian score number (from table 3) along the vertical axis (the left portion of the graph, or y-axis if you remember high school math). You then locate your Practicing Christian score number (from table 4) along the horizontal axis (x-axis, or the bottom portion of the graph). To identify the type of Christian you are, look at the intersection of the two points (believing and practicing). The quadrant in which the intersection exists is the type of Christian you are. The following are a few examples to help illustrate the process:

- **Bob:** Let's say Bob scored a 24 in the first exercise and a 40 in the second, giving him a total Believing Christian score of 64. Bob then had a total score of 52 for the Practicing Christian exercise. Finding the point of intersection of 64 along y-axis and 52 along the x-axis identifies Bob as being a *Laboring Christian.*

- **Sally:** Sally completed the exercise and came up with a combined score of 50 for the Believing Christian portion (y-axis) and 28 for the Practicing Christian portion (x-axis), identifying Sally as a *Hesitant Christian.*

- **Roger:** Roger completed the exercise and was surprised to find that he scored 40 for the Believing Christian portion (y-axis) and 22 for the Practicing Christian portion (x-axis), identifying Roger as an *Adequate Christian.*

- **Diane:** Diane reluctantly completed the exercise and learned she was in rare territory with a combined score of 24 for parts one and two and 58 for part three, identifying her as an unlikely *Latent Christian (defined in the next section).*

- **Bill:** Bill has struggled with his faith for the last year or two and scored a 20 for the believing attributes and a 30 for the practicing attributes, profiling him as a *Departing Christian.*

EXPANDED DESCRIPTIONS OF THE FIVE CHRISTIAN TYPES

Departing Christian

If the exercise identified you as a Departing Christian, you have quite a bit of work to do in reaching your God-given potential as a disciple of Christ. The good news is that the word "departing" is used because the decisions you are currently making are not permanent, thus the "-ing" instead of the "-ed." As a Departing Christian, you are no longer converted (Matthew 18:3), you are more out than in as a Christian (Acts 7:51), and you have become hard hearted (Ephesians 4:18).

As a Departing Christian, you can change your wayward direction by asking for the help of God, who will be quick to answer (Matthew 7:7). Should you resist conversion in Jesus Christ, however, the transformation to counteract the darkness that is pulling you away will be difficult. Don't despair—many in America share your Christian profile, some who don't care and have no intention of improving, and others who truly want to improve. The fact that you are on this expedition says you are one who wants to improve. The Lord is with you!

Adequate Christian

If the exercise identified you as an Adequate Christian, you are currently in the mainstream of Christianity in America today. As an Adequate Christian you are profiled in various studies and publications as being a Christian Atheist, Cultural Christian, Nominal Christian, or a Casual Christian. Each of these terms is essentially the same, describing you as one who believes in Jesus Christ but falls short of practicing what you profess to believe.

As an Adequate Christian, you probably believe what you are doing as a Christian is "good enough" and therefore have no reason to exercise additional faith unto works. As an Adequate Christian, you are lukewarm and nonchalant in your approach to works and nominal in your attitude toward Christ. You likely relish in biblical passages relating to being saved by grace, feeling justified in your lackadaisical approach to practicing Christianity as an active servant of God. Adequate Christians may rationalize they are not goats, but sheep who praise God but have not served him fully (Matthew 25:31–46). As an Adequate Christian, you believe the building of the kingdom of God on earth is the responsibility of others, and you perhaps plan to wait until the eleventh hour to labor, hoping to receive the same wage as those who have labored since the beginning of the day (Matthew 20:1–16).

Adequate Christians are Believing Christians who lack the conviction of faith to become a Practicing Christian—you are stuck somewhere in the middle and believe what you are doing is sufficient. Adequate Christians don't comprehend the wisdom of the adage "use it or lose it" and its relationship to the servant who buried his talent and was cast out (Matthew 25:14–30). You might proclaim to others that you would be the Good Samaritan in the parable from the Bible (Luke 10:30–37), but in reality you would probably be more like the priest and Levite in passing over the poor and needy in the community.

As an Adequate Christian, you have so much potential that can be unleashed to your benefit and the benefit of others. You might do well to begin by considering the admonition of Paul, who wrote, "now it is high time to awake out of sleep: for now is our salvation nearer than when we believed" (Romans 13:11). In other words, you have so much to experience and offer as a Christian, but to do so, you need to snap out of the zombie state you are in. Wake up and get moving!

Hesitant Christian

If the exercise identified you as a Hesitant Christian, then you are one who has all the gifts necessary to make a difference in the world—you simply need to start putting that strong faith of yours to work with a little more practice.

The potential of all Practicing Christians in building and nurturing the kingdom of God on earth is enormous. Jesus Christ taught his disciples, "Verily, verily, I say unto you, He that believeth on me, the works that I do shall he do also; and greater works than these shall he do" (John 14:12). This means that with faith in Christ, your potential is limitless. As a Hesitant Christian, you are blessed with great faith but are routinely operating below your spiritual potential, therefore not living up to the principle of "where much is given much is required" (Luke 12:48).

You have the gift of the Holy Ghost (1 Corinthians 6:19–20), have been blessed with spiritual experiences, and know when to lend a hand and make the sacrifices necessary to glorify God in service. The Hesitant Christian is who Paul had in mind when he wrote, "Now unto him that is able to do *exceeding abundantly above all that we ask or think*, according to the power that worketh in us, Unto him be glory in the church by Christ Jesus throughout all ages" (Ephesians 3:20–21, emphasis added). You may at times be "weary in well doing" (2 Thessalonians 3:13) and miss service opportunities presented by the Lord despite having the "several ability" given to you by your Heavenly Father (Matthew 25:15).

Approach your spiritual potential by exercising the faith you are blessed with and serve the Lord by serving others. The impact you have can be life changing and society altering, and the changes you have to make to realize a greater spiritual potential will be exciting and incredibly fulfilling.

Laboring Christian

If the exercise identified you as a Laboring Christian, you are a rare breed among the disciples of Christ. As a Laboring Christian, you are anxiously endeavoring and actively striving to live the admonition of Christ in emulating his example. In short, you are an exemplary Christian that many can look up to.

Laboring Christians have cultivated resilient and solid faith through practicing what they believe, recognize their blessings, and are unafraid to do what is required in building and nurturing the kingdom of God. They are intimately familiar with and regularly follow the promptings of the Holy Ghost—especially promptings that call for sacrifice in the service of others. Being familiar with the scriptures and having put to the test the admonitions of the Lord, you feel peace and joy in living a life of humility. You pattern your life after the Savior's. The influence a Laboring Christian can have on a society is colossal.

Even Laboring Christians have room for improvement, however. Jesus Christ taught, "But he that shall endure unto the end, the same shall be saved" (Matthew 24:13). While you may be a strong Laboring Christian today, it will be a challenge not to become complacent and instead continuously strengthen your testimony and endure to the end. Life is not static, and you will have challenges that will test your faith and good works. Look for those areas that you can improve in order to reinforce your spiritual armor (Ephesians 6:11).

Latent Christian

If the exercise identified you as a Latent Christian, then you are truly a rarity—one who has a spiritual profile that is a bit backward! The scriptures suggest there are individuals who have faith without works and those with works without faith—you are the latter, but one who has a little bit of faith and an abundance of works. While the spiritual state you are in is helping to build the kingdom of God through good works, you need to grow your faith commensurate to those works or eventually you will spiritually collapse.

As a Latent Christian, you fall outside the evolution of the common Christian journey. For example, for a Laboring Christian to become a Latent Christian, he or she would have to continue in works while losing his or her faith—not a likely scenario. The Hesitant Christian would have to decrease faith while increasing works—also not a likely scenario. So the question becomes how you arrived at this juncture of your Christian journey with your good works outpacing your faith.

Latent Christians are really Laboring Christians-in-waiting. Once you understand and apply faith in your life, you can be born again, transformed, and experience the power and purpose of gospel-centered works. As a Latent Christian, you are a good person whose heart is being purified, whose intentions are righteous, and whose attitude is unselfish. The beauty of being a Latent Christian is that you've already accepted and actively live the principle of sacrifice, a tenet that keeps many Hesitant Christians from reaching their potential as Laboring Christians. Now is the time for you to focus on your faith.

Diary of Thoughts

What type of Christian were you profiled to be?

What surprises you most about your Christian Profile?

When you read the description of your Christian type, what rings most true?

CHARTING A COURSE FOR CHRISTIAN IMPROVEMENT

Now that you know what type of Christian you are, you're in a better position to understand your spiritual inventory at a more detailed level. Keep those exercise scores handy—we will go through each one to understand where your strengths and weaknesses are and help you chart a course for Christian improvement. By charting this spiritual course, you are taking the first step toward greater happiness by becoming the disciple the Lord has enabled and wants you to be. Christ promises us that being yoked with him makes life easier (Matthew 11:30), but to do so requires us to put forth some effort of our own. Let's get moving to the next phase of your spiritual expedition.

Chapter 2

GOD-GIVEN CHRISTIAN POTENTIAL

You now understand what type of Christian you are and what that means. The next phase of your expedition will be charting a course for Christian improvement to help you become the disciple the Lord Jesus Christ wants you to be. However, before charting that course, you need to answer a key question: What is your God-given Christian (aka: spiritual) potential?

Christianity is not a journey that requires us to do the most; Christianity is a journey that requires us to do what we are able. Olympic gold medal swimmer Geoffrey Gaberino once said, "The real contest is always between what you've done and what you're capable of doing."

Paul wrote, "I can do all things through Christ which strengtheneth me" (Philippians 4:13). Jesus taught, "With God all things are possible" (Matthew 19:26). This counsel should motivate us to understand God's will for us (our potential) and then to rely on the Lord for the strength to realize it (reaching that potential). Imagine for a moment a world where everyone lives up to the spiritual potential the Lord has endowed them with. What a fantastic thing that would be for individuals, families, churches, communities, and nations! But what is that potential? Let's look to the scriptures to formulate an answer.

EACH ACCORDING TO HIS SEVERAL ABILITY

The parable of the talents in Matthew 25 is a well-known and often quoted scriptural passage. It centers around servants who are given talents (a unit of money that can also metaphorically represent gifts given to us by God) and their stewardship of those talents. The parable is typically understood as an admonition to do the most with what God has given us. Although that is an important lesson, a small, often overlooked phrase in verse 15 sheds light on another significant message in the parable. In this verse, the master is giving talents to each of the servants—one receives five, another two, and the last one receives one talent—"*to every man according to his several ability*" (Matthew 25:15). In other words, each servant had specific abilities, and the number of talents given to him was according to those abilities.

You are given talents by your Heavenly Father according to your "several ability." One person may have an abundance of talents, another only a few. The number of talents and the types of talents are irrelevant; the most important thing for us to comprehend is that whatever talents, gifts, and capabilities God has given us, he has done so fully understanding our potential to manage those gifts. Therefore, our life's potential is that which God has given us and it is up to us, through Him, to figure that out.

Diary of Thoughts

What talents has the Lord given you?

WHERE MUCH IS GIVEN, MUCH IS REQUIRED

The three servants were given talents by the master but not told specifically what to do with them. Each servant made his own decisions in managing the talents given to him. The servant given five talents earned another five talents, and the servant with two talents earned another two talents. It is clear that these two servants were familiar with the principle of "For unto whomsoever much is given, of him shall be much required" (Luke 12:48).

Strong Practicing Christians are much like the servants with five and two talents in thc parable, putting their faith into action to reach the potential given to them by the Lord. This can be referred to as "magnifying one's talents." There is much to do, so few who are willing to do it (Luke 10:2), and so little time to get it done (John 9:4). Whereas Believing Christians are looking to do as little as possible, Practicing Christians are looking to do as much as the Lord is calling them to do. Those endowed with great potential by the Lord are called to do more than those who may have been endowed with less according to their several ability.

Diary of Thoughts

In what ways do you feel you have been given much by the Lord?

SACRIFICE AND REWARDS

In the parable of the talents, a third servant buried his talent and in doing so was cast out. So what did the first two servants in the parables have that the third one did not? One might be tempted to say "know-how," but we know that the master took the servant's ability into account when bestowing the talent. One might say that the third servant was fearful while the first two were not. This may have been true, but those with faith in the Lord do not fear man (Hebrews 13:6). While we can theorize about the differences between the servants, one principle worth focusing on is sacrifice.

The first two servants were willing to sacrifice their time in magnifying the talents given to them, while the third servant was not. In six passages of the New Testament, Jesus Christ is recorded to have taught, "He that findeth his life shall lose it: and he that loseth his life for my sake shall find it" (Matthew 10:39). Those who make sacrifices to put others first and themselves last (Matthew 20:16) will be rewarded (Ephesians 6:7–8). To reach our full spiritual potential requires us to *make sacrifices.* We are in a position to make personal sacrifices every day for friends, family, our church, our community, and even complete strangers. Sacrifices can also come in the form of self-denial, where we make decisions to forego our own personal pleasure and submit to the will of God.

Diary of Thoughts

What kinds of sacrifices are you prepared to make for the Lord and those around you?

Discipleship in the gospel of Jesus Christ is not an invitation to bask in the goodness of salvation only, but rather an invitation to be yoked with and labor alongside the Lord. A yoke is a crossbar with two U-shaped pieces that go around the necks of a pair of animals working in tandem. The Lord invites us to be yoked with him as a pair, sharing the load side-by-side, making the challenges of meeting our spiritual potential a little easier (Matthew 11:28–30).

Diagram 5: Being Yoked with Jesus Christ

Notice that we are not invited to jump on the Savior's back and allow him to take us the entire way (he already fully bore the load of our sins on the cross); rather, he invites us to embark on the journey yoked together because "every man shall bear his own burden" (Galatians 6:5). How blessed we all are to have Jesus Christ by our side—if we only allow him to be there.

LIKE REWARDS FOR DIFFERING ABILITIES AND RESPONSIBILITIES

Another lesson in the parable of the talents teaches the principle of receiving according to one's effort. Verses 20 to 23 of Matthew 25 are an account of the two faithful servants who doubled their talents. Notice that the rewards given to each of them in verses 21 and 23 are exactly the same: "Well done, good and faithful servant; thou hast been faithful over a few things, I will make thee ruler over many things: enter thou into the joy of thy lord" (Matthew 25:23). Despite the fact the first servant was given five talents, and the second servant was given two talents, they both reached their God-given potential and received a like reward.

If you feel you have been given much less than someone else in the way of talents and blessings, keep in mind this does not mean that your reward in heaven will also be much less! This is not about who has the most talents and blessings; this is about reaching the potential that God the Father has given you with the talents and blessings with which you have been endowed. The rewards of doing so are not just eternal—they can also be reaped in this life in the form of the joy we feel in accomplishing righteous endeavors.

Diary of Thoughts

What are some of your accomplishments that came as a result of using gifts you were blessed with from your Heavenly Father?

Diagram 6 summarizes the content of this chapter in what is referred to as the Path of Spiritual Potential. You start along the path by recognizing the gifts God has given you, then progress by putting forth an effort that is commensurate with those gifts and making the sacrifices necessary to magnify them. Your path ends with you being rewarded in this life and the next, taking comfort in the fact that it is not about having the most gifts, but rather using what gifts you do have to reach your God-given potential.

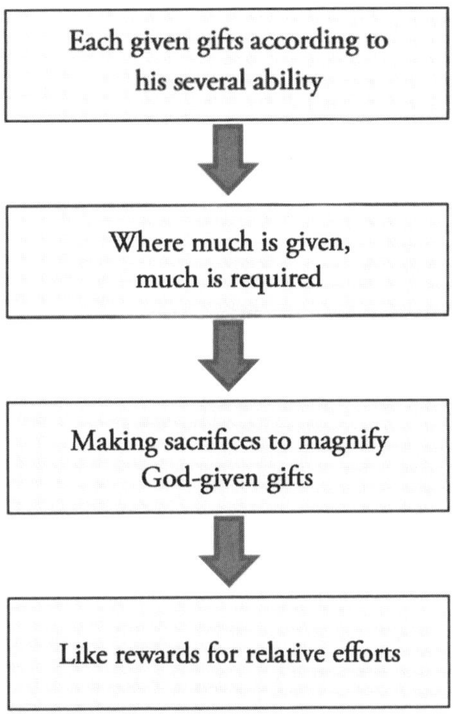

Diagram 6: The Path of Spiritual Potential

Chapter 3

BELIEF ATTRIBUTES EXAMINATION

The Savior said, "I am the vine, ye are the branches," and as branches nourished from the same vine we as individuals are to "*bringeth forth much fruit*: for without me [Jesus Christ] ye can do nothing" (John 15:5, emphasis added). To fully benefit from spiritual nourishment from Jesus Christ, we must first strengthen our faith. Not only faith in the Lord Jesus Christ but also faith in gospel principles and doctrines allow us to understand the Savior more fully. The faith we develop in the whole of the gospel under the influence of the Holy Ghost prepares us to exercise faith in a multitude of other things in life. The Christian Profiling Exercise helps you identify several components of gospel-centered faith that, when studied and applied in your life, will help you develop the faith you need to reach your God-given potential.

The sixteen belief attributes in the exercise are the basic building blocks of Christian faith. As you go through these sixteen attributes, have your answers to the exercise handy by either placing a bookmark in the workbook or having the printouts near you if you completed the exercise online. Record the level of agreement you gave to the statements in the boxes provided for each attribute

THE SIXTEEN ATTRIBUTES OF BELIEF

Jesus Christ–Attributes 1 to 5

The first five attributes of the exercise focus on Jesus Christ as the Savior of the world, the only begotten Son of God, the single source of forgiveness through his infinite sacrifice and resurrection, the giver of everlasting life, and the only way to God the

Father. These beliefs are at the core of Christian faith, helping us understand the divine nature of the Messiah and what he has done for us.

1. **Jesus Christ is the only true Messiah, the Savior of the world:** Jesus confirmed that he is the "Christ, the Son of the living God" (Matthew 16:16; see also Mark 8:29–30 and Luke 9:20–21). To the high priest's question of "Art thou the Christ, the Son of the Blessed?" Jesus responded, "I am" (Mark 14:61-62). The word "Christ" comes from the Greek word *Khristós*, which is a translation of the Hebrew *Māšîaḥ*, meaning the Messiah. The word "messiah" means the anointed one. /5

2. **Jesus Christ is the Only Begotten Son of God:** On numerous occasions Jesus referred to himself as the "son of man," meaning the Messiah in human form. Jesus confirmed he is the Son of God (Luke 22:70 and John 10:36), qualifying he is the "only begotten son" of God in John 3:16-18. This fact was further reinforced by those who testified of the words from God the Father who spoke from heaven , saying, "This is my beloved Son, in whom I am well pleased" (Matthew 3:17; see also Luke 3:22, Mark 1:11, 2 Peter 1:17 and Matthew 17:5). While all believers may become the "sons of God" (John 1:12), there is only one "begotten" son of God—Jesus Christ. /5

3. **Jesus Christ is the only way to the forgiveness of sins:** Jesus proclaimed he has the power to forgive sins (Mark 2:10). Through his agony in the Garden of Gethsemane where his "sweat was as it were great drops of blood" (Luke 22:44), His suffering and death upon the cross (Luke 23:46), and his Resurrection (Mark chapter 16), Jesus overcame physical and spiritual death that we might do the same if we accept him as our personal savior. These three events—the agony in Gethsemane, the suffering and death upon the cross, and the resurrection—are often referred to as the atonement (at-one-ment) of Christ, reconciling man to God. There are denominations of Christianity that accept the atonement as being all three events and some only one. For convenience's sake, we will refer to the Atonement of Christ in this workbook as being this great sacrifice of the Savior. /5

4. **Jesus Christ is the only way to everlasting life (salvation):** According to Jesus Christ one must believe in him to gain eternal life (or everlasting life), otherwise he is condemned (John 3:18). The Savior proclaimed "every one which seeth the Son, and *believeth* on him, may have *everlasting life*: and I will raise him up at the last day" (John 6:40, emphasis added). /5

5. **Jesus Christ is the only way to God the Father:** Jesus said, "I am the way, the truth, and the life: no man cometh unto the Father, but by me" (John 14:6). Similar proclamations made by Jesus include calling himself the "bread of life" (John 6:35) and "the resurrection and the life" (John 11:25). /5

Diary of Thoughts

Which of these belief attributes around Jesus Christ do you struggle with the most, and what are your reservations about it?

What can you do in your everyday life to strengthen your faith in this particular attribute?

God the Father–Attributes 6 to 8

The next three attributes focus on the almighty God, the Father of our spirits, who is one with Jesus Christ and through whom all things are possible. Jesus prayed to the Father that all of us "might know thee the only true God" (John 17:3), giving us the commission to know God the Father in our lives. The Savior continually referred to and glorified his Father in Heaven, calling him his God (John 17:3 and Matthew 27:46), setting the example of how we should do the same in prayer and thanksgiving.

6. **God is our Heavenly Father (the Father of our spirits):** Every mortal human being has a biological father and mother through whom a physical body is obtained. As the sons (and daughters) of God (Hosea 1:10) the spirits of men and women are created by God the Father through a process that is unknown (Hebrews 12:9). This intimate relationship with God the Father is illuminated in the Bible through references to him as "Abba," Aramaic for "father" (Romans 8:15–16). /5

7. **God the Father and Jesus Christ are one:** Jesus said, "I am in the Father, and the Father in me" (John 14:10–11, 20), meaning he is one with God the Father. This was further clarified during Jesus' intercessory prayer when he cried "That they [speaking of his disciples] all may be one; as thou, Father, art in me, and I in thee" (John 17:21–22; see also John 17:11) revealing a perfect oneness between Jesus Christ and God the Father. Christ prayed that we would pattern our own relationships with God after this oneness. /5

8. **God the Father makes all things possible:** Jesus said of our Heavenly Father, "with God all things are possible" (Matthew 19:26). God the Father has all power over heaven and earth and all things in them (Matthew 19:26). His dominion is incomprehensible to man (2 Corinthians 2:14 and Matthew 6:8). /5

Diary of Thoughts

How are you strengthening your relationship or oneness with God your Father?

What can you do to improve your relationship with God your Father?

Holy Ghost–Attributes 9 and 10

The next two attributes focus on the Holy Ghost, which is the Spirit of God that resides and moves within us, illuminating truth and providing comfort to the faithful. While it is God who gives us life and Jesus Christ who redeems us, it is the Holy Ghost who manifests these truths to us and acts as our spiritual GPS.

9. **The Holy Ghost is one with, and proceeds from, God the Father, being active in the lives of the faithful:** The Holy Ghost is a personage of spirit and can manifest himself in various ways—for example, in the form of a dove (Luke 3:21–22). The Holy Ghost communicates directly (spirit-to-spirit) with the spirits of men and women according to his divine will (Acts 13:2, 15:28). The Holy Ghost proceeds from the Father (and the Son in some Christian denominations), for example giving Peter his testimony of Jesus being the Christ (Matthew 16:16–17). While the children of God can witness under the influence of the Holy Ghost that Jesus is the Christ, it is the Holy Ghost alone that testifies of the divinity of Jesus Christ to the hearts of men (1 Corinthians 13:3, 11). /5

10. **The Holy Ghost provides comfort and knowledge from God:** Before he ascended into heaven, Jesus told his apostles that the Holy Ghost (the comforter) would come after his departure (John 16:7). The Holy Ghost is the primary channel from which divine communication flows. The Holy Ghost is the great teacher (John 14:16, 26); he reminds men and women of spiritual truths they have been given (John 14:16); he reveals God's most sacred truths (1 Corinthians 2:9–14); he provides spiritual power (1 Thessalonians 1:5–6); he witnesses on behalf of the Father (Hebrews 10:15); he is the provider of the law (Acts 1:2); and he is the guide and director of the disciples of Christ (Acts 13:4, 16:6). /5

Diary of Thoughts

When have you felt the inspiration of the Holy Ghost in your life?

If the answer to the above question is "never" or you cannot remember, then ponder for a moment how you are living your life and if you are receptive spiritually to the gentle promptings of the Spirit—could you feel and hear him if he were trying to reach you now (if not, why)?

Belief Attributes 11 through 16

11. **All humans suffer from sin, requiring repentance to receive forgiveness:** Repentance is a change of direction, signifying that one is broken and in need of redemption. The only path to redemption is Jesus Christ, whose atoning sacrifice has the power to deliver us through grace from God the Father. Besides urging people to believe in him, Jesus preached repentance, saying, "the kingdom of God is at hand: repent ye, and believe the gospel" (Mark 1:15). The Savior added that unless we repent of our sins we will perish (Luke 13:3–5). /5

Diary of Thoughts

Jesus Christ died for you personally so you can be washed of your sins—how does that make you feel?

12. **Baptism is a spiritual cleansing and gateway into the Church of Jesus Christ:** Baptism is a cleansing from sin and includes a commitment from the baptized to take upon him or herself the name of Jesus Christ, to keep his commandments, and to follow his teachings. With infant baptism, the sponsors make a similar commitment for the baptized. Baptism is the gateway to membership in the Lord's Church and is often followed by receiving the gift of the Holy Ghost. Jesus said, "He that

believeth *and* is baptized shall be saved" (Mark 16:16, emphasis added). Jesus was baptized to fulfill all righteousness (Matthew 3:13–17) and commissioned his disciples to "Go ye therefore, and teach all nations, baptizing them in the name of the Father, and of the Son, and of the Holy Ghost" (Matthew 28:19). /5

Diary of Thoughts

What does your own baptism mean to you today?

If you cannot recall your baptism, or have not been baptized, then how do you think baptism has or can make an impact on your spiritual life?

13. **The Lord's Supper symbolizes a remembrance of Christ's sacrifice if you are a Protestant or a Mormon, or is the literal body and blood of Jesus Christ (Eucharist) if you are a Catholic:** The Lord's Supper (also referred to as the Eucharist, the sacrament, and other terms) symbolizes the sacrifice made by Jesus Christ and the commandment to partake of his body as the bread of life and his blood as the new and everlasting covenant. For Catholics it is not a symbol but rather the literal body and blood of Jesus Christ. Jesus proclaimed, "Whoso eateth my flesh, and drinketh my blood, hath *eternal life*" (John 6:54, emphasis added; see also John 6:51, 53, and 56). Although Jesus does not say partaking of his flesh is a requirement to obtain eternal life, he does make it clear that those who do have eternal life. /5

Diary of Thoughts

How does partaking of the Lord's Supper help you remember Christ's sacrifice?

How has partaking of it made a difference in your life?

14. **The scriptures (for example, Bible) are the inspired word of God:** The scriptures are the inspired word of God. While one can experience all of the aforementioned attributes without the aid of the scriptures, the scriptures accelerate the faith building process. Jesus urged his disciples to "Search the scriptures; for in them ye think ye have eternal life: and they are they which testify of me" (John 5:39). Paul wrote, "All scripture is given by inspiration of God, and is profitable for doctrine, for reproof, for correction, for instruction in righteousness" (2 Timothy 3:16). Although we read the scriptures because we have faith, the scriptures have the power, under the influence of the Holy Ghost, to strengthen our faith.

/5

Diary of Thoughts

How often do you have meaningful experiences with the scriptures?

If you don't read the scriptures regularly on your own, what keeps you from doing so and how can you make a change in your life to commit yourself to spending more time with the inspired word of God?

15. **You are able to believe without seeing in spiritual matters as one having faith (that is, you don't need to be given divine evidence):** The statement from the exercise implies you don't need to be given divine evidence to have faith. It has been said that faith precedes the miracle, meaning miracles only come when one has faith sufficient to receive them. Although the Savior performed miracles during his earthly ministry to help many believe, when we *require* a miracle or a sign, we are embarking on the territory of wickedness (Matthew 16:4). Pure faith focuses on one's ability to live by the words of Paul, who described faith as "the substance of things hoped for, the evidence of things not seen" (Hebrews 11:1). /5

Diary of Thoughts

In what ways do you feel powerful in faith?

In what ways do you feel weak in faith?

16. **You consider yourself to be born again, converted, with a new life in Jesus Christ:** Rebirth, or being born again, centers around conversion and the reality that each one of us must be regenerated in Christ to see the kingdom of God (John 3:3), giving up our former lives to God the Father for a new life in his Son Jesus Christ. /5

Diary of Thoughts

In what ways have you been born again in the Lord Jesus Christ? If you don't feel you have been born again, how can you do so?

Take a moment to reexamine the answers you provided to the sixteen statements regarding these attributes of belief. The ones you scored the lowest on (1, 2, or 3) are the ones you will want to focus on first, allowing the attributes you scored higher on (4 or 5) to be a strength to you in moving forward. Faith is where it all begins, for without faith we cannot please God (Hebrews 11:6) and without faith our works can become dangerously hollow in the sight of God.

Diary of Thoughts

What keeps you from exercising greater faith in your life?

What things or patterns in your life can you change, or what new practices can you implement that will help with the above issue?

Chapter 4

PRACTICE ATTRIBUTES EXAMINATION

THE PATTERN FOR STRENGTHENING YOUR PRACTICES (OR WORKS) RUNS ADJACENT TO, yet slightly behind, the strengthening of faith (as faith is an important prerequisite of works). The sixteen practicing attributes found in part three of the Christian Profiling Exercise are the core works of the Practicing Christian and do not have a logical progression. The recognition of each of these attributes opens the eyes and the heart of the willing and paves the way for committed discipleship in the gospel of Christ. The following is a review of the sixteen attributes. Record the level of agreement you gave to the statements in the boxes provided for each attribute:

1. **You strive to keep all of the commandments of God and the teachings of his Son Jesus Christ:** Samuel the prophet wrote, "to obey is better than sacrifice" (1 Samuel 15:22). Jesus spoke plainly when he told his followers, "If ye love me, keep my commandments" (John 14:15). The commandments of Christ reach far beyond the classic Ten Commandments and include such admonitions as loving one another (John 13:34) and preaching the gospel (Matthew 28:18–20). By keeping the commandments, you will cultivate individual obedience and love for the Savior—both valuable characteristics of a committed disciple of Christ. /5

Diary of Thoughts

How well do you really know the commandments?

What is the most difficult part of keeping the commandments for you?

What can you change in your life to improve your obedience and better demonstrate your love for Jesus Christ?

2. **You regularly repent, asking for forgiveness of and turning away from sin:** Repentance is a prerequisite to baptism. As humans we are prone to sin—sins of commission (things we do) and sins of omission (things we don't do). Because of this tendency, we need to repent regularly (Acts 3:19). Repentance becomes a practicing attribute when regularly performed, helping to develop humility, a contrite spirit, and, most important, a forgiveness of sins. /5

Diary of Thoughts

How often do you fall to your knees to repent of even small wrongdoings in your life?

What keeps you from doing so more often?

3. **You regularly pray to God the Father—out loud, in private, and/or even within your heart:** It is critical that you regularly communicate with your Father in Heaven, offering gratitude for blessings large and small, expressing heartfelt and righteous desires, and receiving personal revelation (Philippians 4:6). Jesus taught

we should pray always (Luke 18:1), having faith that our prayers will be answered (Matthew 21:22). /5

Diary of Thoughts

How often do you pray to your Heavenly Father?

How could you improve your personal prayers?

4. **You strive to follow the teachings and example of Jesus Christ:** To be a disciple of Jesus Christ, one must know the teachings of the Savior (Matthew 5:1–16, Matthew 6:5–6, Matthew 7:1–8, Matthew 22:36-40, Matthew 25:41–45, and so on.) and the example he left for us to emulate (John 13:15). In following Christ we become more like him (1 John 2:6). /5

Diary of Thoughts

What does following Christ mean to you and how do you strive to follow Christ in your life?

5. **You regularly make meaningful personal sacrifices in living the gospel of Jesus Christ:** Christ taught, "If any man will come after me, let him deny himself, and take up his cross *daily*" (Luke 9:23, emphasis added). Notice the scripture says *daily*—not yearly, monthly, or weekly! Denying ourselves and taking up our cross means putting

others first and making sacrifices in a variety of forms. When we regularly sacrifice, we become more like the servant Jesus urged us to be (Matthew 23:11).

Diary of Thoughts

What types of sacrifices have you made in the last sixty days that you can offer to the Lord?

What sacrifices are you willing to make in the future?

6. **You regularly perform service for others, spending your own personal time to do so:** Perhaps the most meaningful form of sacrifice is found in serving others—something that pleases God (Hebrews 13:16). When we give our time to lift up, support, and comfort others we are in reality serving the Lord (Matthew 25:40). James defined "pure religion" as visiting the fatherless and the widows (James 1:27). The easiest place to start serving others is often in our own family (1 Timothy 5:8). /5

Diary of Thoughts

Who can you serve in your life, and what can you do for them?

7. **You regularly share the gospel of Jesus Christ with others:** Christ commissions us all to share the gospel with everyone (Mark 16:15), and this commission was reinforced after his ascension (2 Timothy 4:2). Both the preparation to share (1 Peter 3:15) and the actual act of sharing the gospel strengthen your personal testimony, bring joy to others, open the doors of salvation (Romans 10:10), and express your love for God and your neighbor in a unique and sacred way. /5

Diary of Thoughts

How comfortable are you with sharing the gospel of Jesus Christ with others?

If you are not comfortable sharing the gospel, what do you need in order to feel more comfortable sharing the good news of Jesus Christ?

How will you work toward this goal?

8. **You strive to be pure in heart including earnest attempts to exercise humility, having gratitude in the Lord:** The pure in heart are blessed (Matthew 5:8), have an attitude of gratitude to the Lord (Colossians 3:17), and exercise humility and good works for the glory of God. They also demonstrate charity (1 Timothy 1:5) and the love of others (1 Peter 1:22). Striving to become pure in heart will aid you in your quest to perfect the other fifteen practicing attributes. /5

Diary of Thoughts

How often in prayer do you thank your Heavenly Father for all he has done for you?

Taking one minute, how many things can you identify that you are thankful for as blessings that have come to you from your Heavenly Father?

9. **You regularly give of your time, talents, and substance to others:** Associated with but not the same as attribute six (serving others) relates to giving. Everyone has something to give in the effort to build and nurture the kingdom of God. For some it is money, for others it may be one or more talents, and for still others it may be their time in large or small quantities (Luke 11:41). Giving up the things that are most valuable to you is critical to your spiritual growth and salvation (Matthew 19:21). Sharing your means with others, especially anonymously (Matthew 6:4), brings abundant blessings to both the giver and the receiver. /5

Diary of Thoughts

How do you give of yourself to others?

What are some new ways that you can give of yourself to others in the future?

10. **You regularly praise God and his Son Jesus Christ in worship:** The word "praise" appears in 266 passages of the Bible and the word "worship" appears 175 times—sometimes they even appear together (for example, in Psalm 138:2). Regular praise and worship cultivate meekness through our acknowledgement of our nothingness and by the expression of our gratitude and love for God the Father and his Son Jesus Christ. /5

Diary of Thoughts

What things do you do to praise and worship the Lord daily?

What things do you do on a weekly basis? Monthly? Annually?

11. **You strive to love others in kindness and charity:** You would be right to point out that many of the aforementioned attributes are directly correlated with loving one's neighbor. However, overlapping lessons were a hallmark of the public ministry of Christ, demonstrating the need for constant reinforcement of key gospel

principles. One of the most important principles, second only to loving God, is to love one's neighbor (Luke 10:27), or as Jesus put it so directly "love one another" (John 15:12). /5

Diary of Thoughts

How do you show love for the people within your realm of influence?

12. **You strive to be a good example of Christian values and living:** The most effective way to share the gospel is to be a good example of living the gospel. Paul urged the disciple of Christ to "be thou an example of the believers, in word, in conversation, in charity, in spirit, in faith" (1 Timothy 4:12). The Savior taught, "Let your light so shine before men, that they may see your good works, and glorify your Father which is in heaven" (Matthew 5:16). Vigilance in being a good example will purify your thoughts and actions, strengthening you as a Christian. /5

Diary of Thoughts

In what ways can you be a better example of a believer to others?

13. **You regularly read and study the scriptures (for example, the Bible):** Having faith that the scriptures are the inspired word of God is important, but it is even more important that you regularly study the scriptures. Paul counseled "All scripture is given by inspiration of God, and is profitable for doctrine, for reproof, for correction, for instruction in righteousness" (2 Timothy 3:16). The value of the scriptures in our lives as Christians is so great that it caused Jesus to tell his disciples to "*Search the scriptures*; for in them ye think ye have eternal life: and they are they which testify of me" (John 5:39, emphasis added). Searching implies a sense of urgency, as opposed to scanning or simply looking something over. /5

Diary of Thoughts

How often do you open your scriptures and read for more than just a minute or two?

What are ways you can improve your commitment to, and actually following through with, searching the scriptures regularly so as to understand and know Jesus Christ and his gospel more fully?

14. **You regularly fellowship with other Christians in worship:** When a piece of coal is in a fire, it gives off heat and transfers heat to and from the other coals in the fire. When that same coal is removed from the fire, it will burn hot for a short period and then become cold until it is once again placed back into the fire. Fellowshipping allows disciples of Christ to give spiritual and tangible support to, while obtaining spiritual support from, other Christians with whom they worship and socialize. It's essential that a Christian both give and receive spiritual strength. John wrote that fellowship brings believers together with the Father and his Son Jesus Christ (1 John 1:3). Fellowship can include fun, wholesome activities where prayer and uplifting, Christ-centered conversation abound (Matthew 18:20). /5

Diary of Thoughts

What are ways you can increase your fellowshipping in order to spiritually strengthen yourself and lift up others?

15. **You strive to actively forgive and show mercy to others:** You will, at one point or another, be offended by the words or actions of another. The offense may come from family, friends, strangers, and even church leaders. Jesus taught we are required to forgive them all—regardless of the severity of their transgression against us and regardless of the number of times they offend (Matthew 18:22). We are called to be merciful just as our Father in Heaven is merciful (Luke 6:36). Extending forgiveness to others brings spiritual growth, peace of mind, humility, and, most important, mercy from our Heavenly Father for our own transgressions (Matthew 5:7).

/5

Diary of Thoughts

Who do you need to forgive in order to let go of ill feelings that are inhibiting your spiritual growth in Christ?

16. **You strive to be a peacemaker among those with whom you associate:** Peacemakers promote peace; however, they can also be defined as those who share the good news (that is, the gospel) with others, bringing them peace. Being a peacemaker requires patience, love, understanding, compassion, and a desire for peace, all of which are characteristics of the Savior, who said, "Blessed are the peacemakers: for they shall be called the children of God" (Matthew 5:9).

/5

Diary of Thoughts

In what ways are you a peacemaker?

Take a moment to reexamine the answers you provided to the sixteen statements regarding these attributes of practice. The ones you scored the lowest on (1, 2, or 3) are the ones you will want to focus on first, allowing the attributes you scored higher on (4 or 5) to be a strength to you in moving forward. Practice, or works, is manifest in a Christian according to their faith. As James so aptly counseled all of us, "faith without works is dead" (James 2:20, 26, and 17).

Diary of Thoughts

What keeps you from exercising greater works in your life?

SUMMARIZING THE BELIEVING AND PRACTICING ATTRIBUTE EXERCISE

The thirty-two attributes—sixteen relating to faith (believing) and sixteen relating to works (practicing)—can easily overwhelm even the strongest of Christians. Remember, spiritual growth is a journey and not a destination. The prophet Isaiah taught "precept upon precept . . . line upon line; here a little, and there a little" (Isaiah 28:10).

As the tortoise from one of Aesop's Fables taught us, "Slow and steady wins the race."

We are all a work in progress on earth, continually laboring on these things with continuous improvement, not overnight perfection, as our goal. You may improve only a little day to day, but that is all that is required to make a difference in your life and the lives of those around you. Small incremental improvements will help you reach your spiritual potential and arrive safely in the mansions of the Lord in the life hereafter. It takes desire and commitment to stay on the narrow path and the road map provided here is meant to strengthen on your journey as a disciple of Christ.

Diary of Thoughts

When considering your belief score of ____ and practice score of ____ on this date ____________________; where do you want to be one year from now?

Belief: ________

Practice: ________

What type of Christian would these scores profile you as a year from now?

What changes in your life do you need to make in order to reach this spiritual goal in the next year?

Chapter 5

THE DYNAMICS OF FAMILY

EVERY INDIVIDUAL BORN ON EARTH IS PART OF A FAMILY. IDEALLY THAT FAMILY CONsists of a mother, father, siblings, and extended members (aunts, uncles, cousins, and so on). Far too often, however, families fall short of that ideal, resulting in single-parent families, families where there is no parent present at all, families with two mothers or fathers, and every other variety.

FAMILY FROM A BIBLICAL PERSPECTIVE

The Bible provides stories of close-knit blood-related families such as Mary, Martha, and Lazarus (John 11); close in-laws such as Ruth and Naomi (Ruth 1:16); dysfunctional families like that of King David (2 Samuel 11–13) and Jacob with his twelve sons (Genesis 34–37); and even families where one brother murders another like Cain and Abel (Genesis 4:8). It is comforting to know that the families of the Bible were not perfect! Fantastic families can raise troubled kids and troubled families can raise fantastic kids. Whatever the case, families make an impact on all of us.

Parents within a Family

The establishment of the family in the Bible begins shortly after the creation of Adam. "The Lord God said, It is not good that the man should be alone; I will make him an help meet for him" (Genesis 2:18), marking the beginning of marriage between a man and a woman as "one flesh" (Matthew 19:4–6). In this sacred relationship husbands are urged to "love your wives, even as Christ also loved the church, and gave himself for it" (Ephesians 5:25). This bond between husband and wife is so central to the gospel that Paul wrote, "neither is the man without the woman, neither the woman without the man, in the Lord" (1 Corinthians 11:11).

Children within a Family

From the marriage between a man and a woman comes children, which "are an heritage of the Lord" (Psalm 127:3). Children are called upon to "honour thy father and thy mother" (Exodus 20:12) and to "obey your parents in the Lord" (Ephesians 6:1; see also Colossians 3:20). Children are counseled to "hear the instruction of thy father, and forsake not the law of thy mother" (Proverbs 1:8; see also Proverbs 6:20), calling a son (or daughter) wise in making his father glad or a son foolish in despising his mother (Proverbs 15:20).

Parents in turn are counseled to "provoke not your children to wrath: but bring them up in the nurture and admonition of the Lord" (Ephesians 6:4). If a parent will "Train up a child in the way he should go . . . when he is old, he will not depart from it." (Proverbs 22:6). Parents are called upon to provide for the temporal needs of their "own house" and even those relatives that are not of the household (1 Timothy 5:8).

Given the importance of the family, how can Christians strengthen their family collectively while strengthening members of the family individually?

STRENGTHENING THE FAMILY: THE DIVINE TRIANGLE

Strengthening a family, and the individuals within the family, starts with what is referred to as the "Divine Triangle." The lesson of the Divine Triangle is that the closer individuals in a family come to Jesus Christ, the closer they become to one another. Nowhere is this truer than with the husband and wife, who are the patriarch and matriarch of the family and the glue that holds a righteous family together. Consider the following diagram:

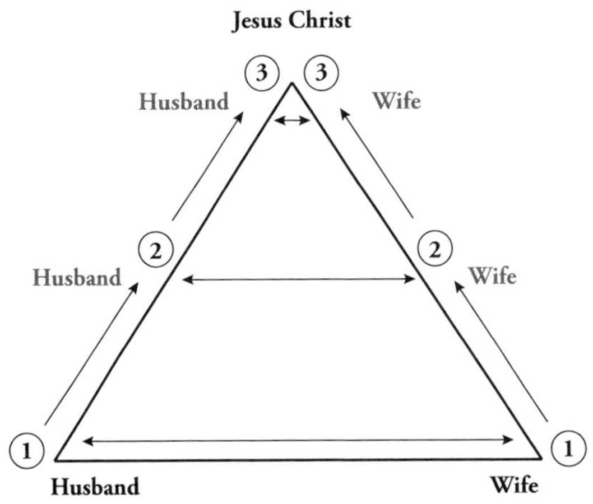

Diagram 7: The Divine Triangle

The husband and wife begin at opposites sides of the base (the circles with the number 1 in them) with Jesus Christ at the apex. As the husband and wife individually move closer to Jesus Christ along the legs of the triangle toward the apex (points 1, 2, and 3), the distance between them becomes smaller and smaller. The closer they become to Jesus Christ as individuals (according to the attributes discussed in the previous chapter—especially love), the closer they become as man and wife in unity with the Savior.

The Divine Triangle can be adapted to put any two individuals or groups at the base, such as a brother and a sister, a son and the rest of the family, a daughter and a mother, and so forth. The result is the same in any case. As the individuals or groups strive to be more devoted to the Savior, they will become more unified with one another as well. Conceptually, the Divine Triangle can be turned ninety degrees one way or the other, putting Jesus Christ and another individual or group at the base, with a particular individual or group at the top. This can be done to *symbolically* represent those at the base supporting and strengthening the individual or group at the top. Sometimes one person in the family, or even the entire family itself, needs a little more reinforcement, and in those instances Jesus Christ and one or more family members can be at the base of the Divine Triangle to hold them up. In this case the Divine Triangle becomes an inspired pillar of support for the individual or group at the apex.

Diary of Thoughts

How does your family impact your relationship with Jesus Christ?

What can you do to help your family become more centered on Christ?

PRACTICING HEALTHY FAMILY DYNAMICS

Focusing on spiritual aspects to strengthen the family is important, but it is not the only lesson to learn here. Books such as Stephen R. Covey's *The Seven Habits of Highly Effective Families* and articles such as "Experts Reveal the Key Ingredients to a Happy Family Life," written by Denise Mann for WebMD, offer practical advice to families on managing the day-to-day dynamics of family living. The common element in these works is that they advocate spending time together in wholesome activities, listening to one another, and building trust among family members.

The formation of a strong family begins and ends with a commitment to the gospel of Jesus Christ, but it also involves the consistent application of tried-and-true principles that allow families to experience the joys associated with being unified in the Savior.

Chapter 6

THE DYNAMICS OF CHURCH

STRONG INDIVIDUALS AND STRONG FAMILIES SHOULD MAKE FOR A STRONG CHURCH; however, that is not always the case. Bringing together two or more strong families full of righteous individuals does not guarantee a unified congregation where the whole is greater than the sum of its parts. The lesson behind this unfortunate reality can be illustrated with food. A thick, juicy steak is a favorite of many, as is a good bowl of ice cream; however, steak à la mode is not likely to be a winning menu item. Taking the analogy further, it is common to use bleach to clean tile grout, purify water, and whiten clothes. Ammonia is likewise useful for cleaning. However, mix bleach and ammonia together and the result is toxic, even deadly.

Our church "family" is important to our spiritual growth because it provides a method and place of worship, other Christians to fellowship with, and a platform of education, to name just a few of the benefits. Being able to maximize our church experiences as members, or, if you're a leader, being able to help members maximize their church experiences, should be a primary objective of any faith community.

THE CHURCH AS THE BODY OF CHRIST

In the twelfth chapter of Paul's first letter to the Corinthians, he addresses the diversity of spiritual gifts and the various positions within the church. In verses 12 to 27, Paul provides a long and detailed analogy of different parts of a body and how they work together as one. To fully appreciate the importance and power of this counsel, you can break each verse down to understand how it applies to you and your congregation. Let's use verses 12 through 14 as examples:

Verse 12: "*For as the body is one, and hath many members, and all the members of that one body, being many, are one body: so also is Christ.*" Your church operates like a single body that has many parts, each working together, and together that church is one in Christ.

Verse 13: "*For by one Spirit are we all baptized into one body, whether we be Jews or Gentiles, whether we be bond or free; and have been all made to drink into one Spirit.*" The members of your church may come from different backgrounds, but you have all been inspired by and partake of the same spirit together.

Verse 14: "*For the body is not one member, but many.*" Your church is not just one but many persons, including you.

Paul went through this highly detailed analogy to reinforce that every member of the church is valuable and necessary to create a strong and edifying church that has Christ at its head. Diagram 8 illustrates how the members of a congregation make up the body of Christ. There are almost a limitless number of members in various positions that could be shown here, each one linked directly to Christ from a spiritual perspective.

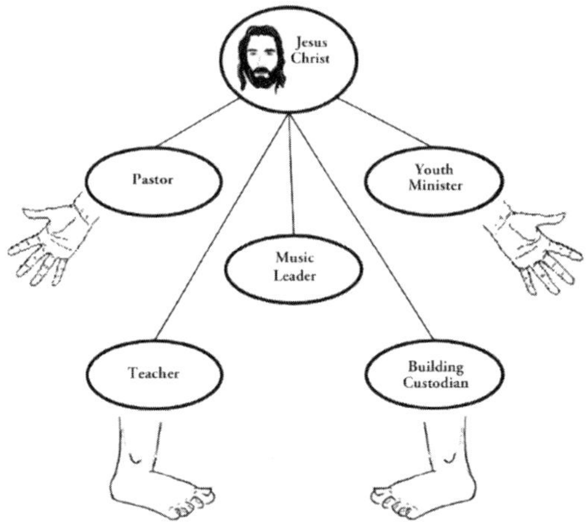

Diagram 8: The Church as the Body of Christ

Paul doesn't use this analogy in his letter to the Corinthians alone; he also employs it in his letter to the Ephesians (Ephesians 1:22–23) and to the Romans (Romans 12:4). Paul believed strongly in the concept of the Body of Christ.

Diary of Thoughts

How do you see yourself as a member of the Body of Christ?

If you do not see yourself as a member of the Body of Christ, why not?

THE THINGS THAT WEAKEN AND DIVIDE THE CHURCH

A number of things that can divide a congregation at the member level include, but are not limited to, the following:

- **Politics**: Few things stir up passionate emotion and immediate response as much as the words "conservative" and "liberal." In the modern era there are real and perceived connections and ideals attributed to these explosive labels as they relate to spiritual matters. Politically speaking, the reality is that Christianity is full of both conservatives and liberals, creating a fanatical division among those who choose to allow politics to divide them (and in so doing divide the Body of Christ).

- **Social Issues**: The two social issues that divide Christians most deeply are abortion and homosexuality. There isn't room enough in a hundred books to resolve the chasms caused by these issues. We must manage these issues in the same way that the Christian world must treat theological differences among denominations: passionate disagreements are going to happen, but the most productive path is to locate and build upon common values instead.

- **Sin/Pride**: Sin separates man from God (Isaiah 59:2) and divides members from one another. The sin that does so most prevalently is pride. Pride is considered one of the "seven deadly sins" and "is the commencement of all sin," according to Saint Augustine. Pride is toxic, attacking congregational unity and sickening the assembly like swift-moving bacteria in the Body of Christ. Pride is individual in nature, but it can spread to groups, creating cliques within churches that are lethal and corrosive.

- **Racism and Other Forms of Prejudice**: One might think racism and prejudice would be the last thing a Christian could be stricken with, but both are alive and well in the hearts of many Christians today. Racism and prejudice divide Christians in a way that is entirely pointless and completely contrary to the gospel. Nonetheless, societal norms have bred racism and prejudice over the centuries, making it a strong element of American culture, and one that has been difficult to eliminate entirely.

- **Culture**: Cultural differences among people do not appear to be formidable on the surface but—underneath ethnic and social differences—can be significant. For example, a southern conservative Protestant of black African descent accustomed to certain practices of worship may not be comfortable in the same church in upstate New York where cultural norms are different. A native Latin American Catholic is probably accustomed to a certain pace and style of church services that is significantly different than those found among Catholic churches in Middle America.

- **Ministerial Conflicts:** Many Christian churches have a ministry that includes more than one pastor or set of leaders. There are assistant pastors, counselors, youth leaders, and other individuals in the ministry who fill important roles of leadership. When there is a lack of solidarity among church leaders, members may choose to align themselves along leadership lines, creating division within the church.

- **Generational Differences:** Differences have always existed between generations in language, attitudes, and the application of technology. From a spiritual standpoint, these generational differences can be magnified when youth begin to feel that the church no longer speaks to them and they are unable to relate to the doctrines, practices, and principles of the gospel as taught in a particular congregation.

- **Gender Conflicts:** An issue easily ignored that can divide spiritual communities is gender. Churches allow gender to divide when one sex exerts unrighteous dominion over another, either individually or as a group.

- **Personality Conflicts:** Although it may seem trite to some, personality conflicts cannot only be divisive, but explosive. Personality conflicts can arise between two or more people and be as simple as one party being logical and the other being emotional, or as complex as both parties being on opposite sides of the Myers-Briggs spectrum. Without recognition and respect for one another's personality types, and the value each can bring to solving problems and dealing with issues, there can be constant clashes and negative consequences overall.

- **Bigotry:** Bigotry is much like racism and other forms of prejudice where intolerance of creeds or beliefs that differ from one's own abound in the heart, impacting outward actions. Bigotry as a religious discriminatory practice is often less cunning than the strategies used by racists or those with extreme prejudice. Bigotry is laced with ignorance, self-centeredness, and a complete absence of the love of God.

These catalysts of church division are ever present, each one holding lethal potential to divide and poison congregations. Ben Franklin observed that "an ounce of prevention is worth a pound of cure." The key is to strengthen members spiritually in a way that helps *prevent* these toxic elements from infiltrating a congregation.

Diary of Thoughts

What are the most divisive things you experience within your church congregation?

STRENGTHENING MEMBERS AND THE CHURCH

Paul, in his model of the Body of Christ, was inspired to understand what motivates mankind in its quest for discipleship in the gospel of Christ. Humans are complex beings but follow basic physiological patterns that, when understood, can help motivate people to reach their full potential as children of God.

Perhaps the most comprehensive model of human psychology was developed by Abraham Maslow in 1943. Maslow found that humans attempt to satisfy their most basic needs first before moving on, in a serial fashion, to more marginal needs. The five levels identified by Maslow are physiological (food, water, and so on), safety (security, employment, and so on), belonging and affection (friendship, family), esteem (achievement, respect of others, and so on), and self-actualization (morality, creativity, and so on). Maslow's "Hierarchy of Needs" is most typically illustrated as a pyramid:

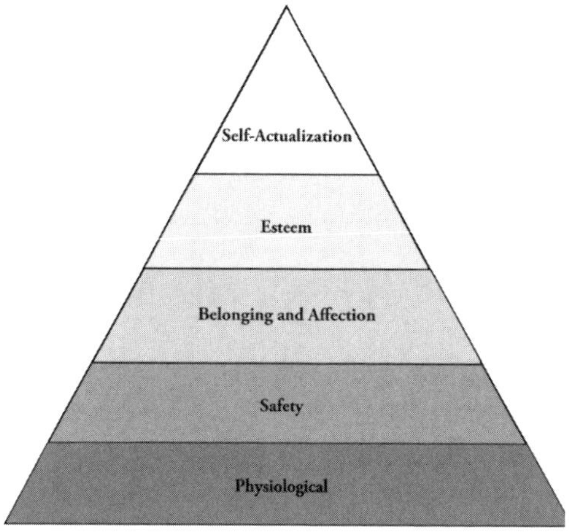

Diagram 9: Maslow's Hierarchy of Needs Model

By considering Paul's teaching on the Body of Christ, along with other gospel principles relating to individuals and the Lord's Church, let's reconfigure Maslow's model to reflect a more church-centered model of human dynamics—we'll call this the Spiritual Hierarchy of Needs model:

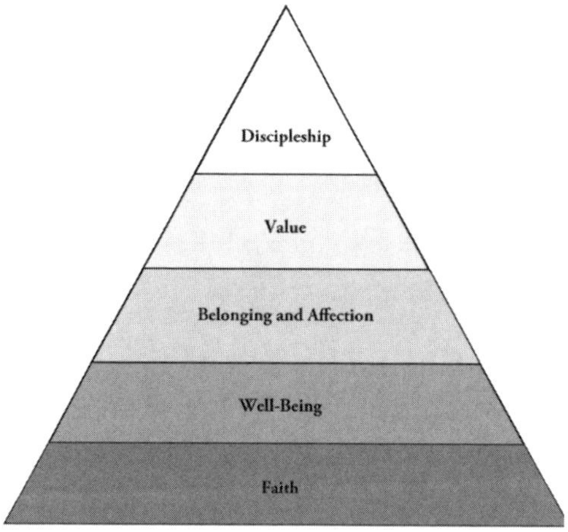

Diagram 10: Spiritual Hierarchy of Needs Model

This "Spiritual Hierarchy of Needs" model closely mirrors Maslow's Hierarchy of Needs in that one level must be satisfied before moving to the next level. In order for the Church to be strengthened, it must create an environment for its members to grow spiritually, thus leading to a synergistic relationship where the whole is more than the sum of the parts (that is, 1 + 1 = 3 or more). Spiritual synergy is achieved when "all things work together for good to them that love God" (Romans 8:28). The levels of the Spiritual Hierarchy of Needs are defined as the following:

- **Faith:** Likened to the physiological level of Maslow's model, faith is the foundation and most basic of all Christian needs leading to rebirth, education, understanding, and the acceptance of gospel truth.
- **Well-Being:** Likened to the safety level of Maslow's model, well-being follows faith and is a search for spiritual hope, confidence, meaningful participation in the assembly, healing of past wrongs, and joy in the love of God.
- **Belonging and Affection:** Likened to the level with the same name in Maslow's model, this level finds the Christian yearning for fellowship among members and feeling like part of a close-knit church family where loyalty and trust abound.
- **Value:** Likened to the Esteem level of Maslow's model, value is the desire to make meaningful contributions to the church family in order to gain the respect of others and feel a righteous sense of pride in being a vibrant member of the Body of Christ.
- **Discipleship:** Likened to the Self-Actualization level of Maslow's model, discipleship is a result of satisfying the previous needs. Discipleship is a need to make a deeper personal commitment to the gospel, to reach one's spiritual potential, to experience sacrifice in taking up one's cross, and to devote one's life—body and soul—as a follower of Jesus Christ.

As church members move up the pyramid of the spiritual hierarchy, they also move from left to right in the Christian Continuum mentioned earlier. The Laboring Christian is likely one who has effectively realized the four bottom components of the Spiritual Hierarchy of Needs and has entered true discipleship in Jesus Christ. On the other side of the spectrum, Departing Christians are likely struggling with faith and well-being. Adequate Christians struggle with well-being along with belonging and affection. Hesitant Christians struggle with value. Knowing each of these individuals personally, church leaders are in a position to understand how to most effectively minister to them along their spiritual hierarchy of needs.

The Spiritual Hierarchy of Needs model integrates the object lesson taught by Paul in the analogy of the Body of Christ regarding the psychology of human nature and the serialization of needs fulfillment. When churches begin focusing more on strengthening individuals and families than on programs and fundraising, the Body of Christ will be strengthened and unified.

Diary of Thoughts

Where do you see yourself on the Spiritual Hierarchy of Needs?

What do you feel you need spiritually—from yourself, from your church, and so on—in order to move more in the direction of discipleship?

Chapter 7

THE DYNAMICS OF COMMUNITY

THE IDEAL SCENARIO IS FOR A COMMUNITY TO BE MADE UP OF STRONG INDIVIDUALS, families, and churches. Unfortunately, because most American Christians are operating under their spiritual potential, most communities in America are operating under their societal potential. A community is defined broadly in this sense and can be local to a neighborhood or encompass an entire nation or even the world. Consider the following societal lineage:

- Individuals make up families
- Families make up neighborhoods
- Neighborhoods make up cities
- Cities make up counties
- Counties make up districts
- Districts make up states
- States make up a nation
- Nations make up the world

This cascade effect of responsibility is sometimes referred to as the doctrine of subsidiarity. If we think in terms of churches—churches made up of individuals such as you—a community can be made up of neighborhood churches, churches around a city, or churches throughout a state or the nation.

THE COMMUNITY AND YOUR CHRISTIANITY

We have learned that the choices you make, your family, and even the church you attend can influence your Christianity. But does your community affect your faith? While the answer could be yes, the more important question is "How much does your Christianity impact your community?" As history has demonstrated (through the works of Martin Luther, Billy Graham, Harriet Beecher Stowe, John Milton, Joan of Arc, Phoebe Palmer, and Galileo Galilei to name a few), one strong Practicing Christian can have a huge effect on a community. And if that's the case, imagine the impact a large group of strong Practicing Christians can have on a community! Emulating the example of the Savior, we as Christians are called to strengthen the community in which we live and can do so in a variety of ways.

STRENGTHENING THE COMMUNITY AS AN INDIVIDUAL

As a Practicing Christian, there is no shortage of ways you can help strengthen your community. There are soup kitchens, homeless shelters, rescue missions, nursing homes, and local schools that are in dire need of volunteers to lend a hand. City organizations are in constant need of help picking up trash along roads, sprucing up parks, and making public areas more presentable. If you desire to make a difference in your community, the key is to not wait around to be asked—take the initiative and make it happen! The woman with an issue of blood (Mark 5:25–34) and the blind beggar (Mark 10:46–52) did not wait around to be healed; they took the initiative to seek out Jesus themselves. Paul warned against idleness and encouraged the believers in Christ to "be not weary in well doing" (2 Thessalonians 3:11–13).

Although the community will surely benefit by your increased involvement, an important by-product of your involvement is how it will benefit you. Jesus counseled that it is better to give than to receive (Acts 20:35) and Paul reminds us that whatever kindness we show to others will be returned to us by the Lord (Ephesians 6:8). We shouldn't serve with the expectation of reward, but rather recognize that the Lord appreciates our love for Him and others and blesses us for our service in the most unexpected of ways.

Diary of Thoughts

What are some ways you can become involved in strengthening your community?

STRENGTHENING THE COMMUNITY AS A CHURCH

An even more effective way of strengthening your community, while at the same time strengthening the Body of Christ within your congregation, is to serve as a church. There is greater strength in numbers (Ecclesiastes 4:9) to accomplish the work. Beyond the positive effect on the community, serving together shoulder to shoulder also builds the muscles of the Church body. All become equal in yoking themselves with the Lord, coming together with the purposes of losing their lives in the service of others. Nothing bonds a congregation more fully than to be joined together in service.

Diary of Thoughts

When was the last time you served with your fellow Church members?

How did it make you feel?

If you have never served with your church as a congregation, in what ways do you believe your church can join together to make a difference in your community?

STRENGTHENING THE COMMUNITY AS A COLLECTION OF CHURCHES

The unifying force that brings together different churches in the community is driven by the spirit of ecumenism. This is a spirit of serving those in need by consolidating the gifts and talents of the community to "minister the same one to another, as good stewards of the manifold grace of God" (1 Peter 4:10). Ecumenism promotes unity among religions through greater cooperation and understanding. Ecumenism is often mistakenly interpreted as two or more denominations coming together to water down each other's beliefs to form a compromised treaty of faith. This is not the objective of true ecumenism. Note that the two key words in the above definition are "cooperation" and "understanding," not "theological amalgamation."

An example of ecumenism might be three neighborhood churches—a Conservative Protestant, a Catholic, and a Mainline Protestant Church—coming together to help renovate a building used to provide meal services to the poor. Such an ecumenical effort focuses on cooperation and does not require theological alignment.

Ecumenism is a bridge-building methodology between churches that would otherwise remain separate, allowing two or more congregations to enjoy expanded fellowship and service with the larger spiritual community. Regarding ecumenism, Billy Graham once said "World travel and getting to know clergy of all denominations has helped mold me into an ecumenical being. We're separated by theology and, in some instances, culture and race, but all that means nothing to me anymore."

The Power of Christian Intra-faith Ministry

When the Savior gave the world a new commandment to "love one another" (John 13:34) and exclaimed the poor were blessed (Luke 6:20), the door was opened to serving those less fortunate, adding, "For ye have the poor always" (Matthew 26:11). The act of multidenominational service within the same religion is called intra-faith ministry.

Love in the Name of Christ (Love INC) as an Intra-faith Example

Nestled in the Douglas County Lakes Area of Minnesota is the organization Love in the Name of Christ, or Love INC. Love INC networks local Christian church ministries and volunteers, across denominations, to serve the needs of their local community. Love INC mobilizes Christians to work together, with help from community organizations and government resources, to provide coordinated help to the poor—both spiritually and temporally. As of 2012 there were nearly thirty different Love INC member churches across various Christian denominations including Roman Catholic, Lutheran, Methodist, Presbyterian, and non-denominational.

In June and July of 2011, Love INC assisted 38 families through 187 hours of volunteer service in Douglas County. This may seem small, but consider the impact of such an intra-faith Christian ministry over several months, a year, or a decade. These efforts start small and inspire other efforts in local communities as Christians from various faith traditions come together in the work of the Lord.

The Power of Interfaith Ministry

Serving the poor is the responsibility of people of all faith traditions—including those who are not Christian. Ecumenism can reach far beyond Christianity in working together with people of non-Christian faiths to strengthen communities and help those in need. These efforts are often referred to as interfaith ministry. Multidenominational organizations have access to more resources, a wider reach into neighborhoods, and a greater appreciation for the variation of spiritual cultures. Outside of helping those in need (which is the priority), the by-products of interfaith efforts are increased community unity, the opportunity to bear witness of Christ through example (and, as appropriate, through word), and a strengthening of the Body of Christ.

Northwest Assistance Ministries of Houston as an Interfaith Example

In 1983, after being overwhelmed with requests for assistance, one social worker and a local clergyman convinced eight other Christian congregations and one Jewish synagogue to lay aside their theological differences to focus on serving the needy of the 242 square mile Northwest Houston area. This effort gave birth to Northwest Assistance Ministries (NAM). From its modest beginnings of ten congregations and a starting budget of less than $50,000, NAM grew into a force of over fifty congregations and a budget approaching $9 million in 2011, serving a staggering 1.5 million residents. The fifty multidenominational congregations of NAM include Anglican, Assembly of God, Baptist, Catholic, Christian Reformed, Church of Christ, Church of Christ Scientist, The Church of Jesus Christ of Latter-day Saints (LDS/Mormon), Episcopal, Evangelical, Evangelical Lutheran, Jewish, Lutheran, Methodist, Nondenominational, Presbyterian, and Seventy-day Adventist.

In a 2012 interview, Anais Watsky, who was an early member and became the NAM director in 1987, explained that although there were minor concerns with the diversity of theological beliefs, there was never enough concern to deny a willing congregation to enter into the NAM fold. Any desire for doctrinal alignment was relinquished in favor of consolidating precious resources to address the growing needs of Houston-area families.

Diary of Thoughts

What do you think about your church joining with other churches to serve in the community?

What are your feelings toward other Christians who do not share the same beliefs you do?

How would you feel about serving in your community with other Christians who do not share the same beliefs as you?

Chapter 8

RECAPPING THE EXPEDITION

You have come to the end of your expedition and it is time to review where you have been and build an album of your experiences so that the memories remain fresh and vibrant:

- **Chapter 1:** Your first stop was to identify your Christian type along the Christian Continuum and to understand that there are a variety of Christians all around you—each on their own journey and walk with the Lord.
- **Chapter 2:** Next you learned about your spiritual potential and how God has endowed you with spiritual gifts according to his will and his expectation that you magnify those gifts through sacrifice.
- **Chapter 3:** You then explored the sixteen attributes relating to belief and how those attributes can be applied in your life toward a greater faith in Jesus Christ and his gospel.
- **Chapter 4:** Next you read about the sixteen attributes relating to practice and the need for you to put your faith into action by performing good works in the name of the Lord.
- **Chapter 5:** Your expedition then took you into the dynamics of family, how family can impact your spirituality, and how the Divine Triangle can help strengthen families and individuals within your family.
- **Chapter 6:** From family you then turned your attention to church, examining the Body of Christ and how each member of the congregation fills an important role as branches being nourished from the same vine (Christ).
- **Chapter 7:** Your trip concluded by considering the community in which you live and how you and your church can have a positive effect on your community while giving yourself opportunities and experiences to grow spiritually.

The diary of thoughts you have written in this workbook constitute a log of your expedition to which you can refer in the future. It is now time for you to create a final set of journal entries by reflecting for a moment on what you have learned and experienced so far. Close your eyes and try to feel the inspiration of the Holy Ghost as you consider which lessons were of the most worth to you personally.

Diary of Thoughts

What did you learn about yourself that you did not know or realize before?

What changes are you willing to make in your life to become a more dedicated disciple of Christ?

DISCIPLESHIP PLEDGE

I COMMIT MYSELF TO THE LORD JESUS CHRIST AND WILL TRY TO THE BEST OF my ability to understand the spiritual potential I have been endowed with and to live up to that potential in belief and practice through small incremental improvements each day, week, month, and year. I specifically commit myself to regular prayer and scripture reading so that I am able to commune with my Heavenly Father and receive strength and direction under the inspiration of the Holy Ghost and his inspired word. Should I transgress the laws of God, I will seek forgiveness through repentance, which is made possible through the atonement of Jesus Christ. I recognize my imperfections before God and will therefore rely on him, his Only Begotten Son Jesus Christ, and the Holy Ghost each day while doing my part to live up to this pledge. I solemnly make this pledge in the name of Jesus Christ.

Signed ________________________________ Date ______________

FINAL THOUGHTS

Your expedition in this workbook has come to a close, and you can now continue your lifelong spiritual journey in Jesus Christ. Your journey can be a safe and eternally fulfilling one if you look to God the Father as your strength, to Jesus Christ as your guide, and to the Holy Ghost as your GPS. Although the Father, the Son, and the Holy Ghost are there for you, you and your choices will ultimately dictate your path. May your journey be a grand one in our Lord and Savior Jesus Christ. Amen.

ABOUT THE AUTHOR

Eric Shuster has dedicated his writing career to building bridges of understanding between Christians while helping the faithful find a deeper sense of spirituality centered on Jesus Christ. His book *Where are the Christians? The Unrealized Potential of a Divided Religion* uses the classic format of who, what, where, and how to explore Christianity and the dynamics that unite and divide the religion into the unrealized potential it suffers from today. His other books, *Catholic Roots, Mormon Harvest* and *The Biblical Roots of Mormonism* (coauthored with Charles Sale), use the Bible as a common scriptural platform to explore the doctrines of Catholicism and Mormonism and the dynamics of spiritual conversion. With a professional research background, directorship at the Foundation for Christian Studies, and his unique life experiences, Mr. Shuster is able to delve into complex spiritual subject matter and make it understandable and enjoyable to the everyday reader.

Mr. Shuster is a veteran of the information technology industry and has held several executive positions in a variety of business disciplines, including CEO of IntelliClear, a global market research and business strategy firm. Mr. Shuster holds an industrial engineering management degree from San Jose State University and an MBA from the University of Phoenix. Mr. Shuster and his wife, Marilyn, have been married for over twenty-five years and have several biological and adopted children.

NOTES

0 26575 12937 3